THE ACA LEGAL SERIES
Volume 4

"COUNSELING MINOR CLIENTS"

THE ACA LEGAL SERIES

Series Editor: Theodore P. Remley, Jr., JD, PhD

Volume 1 *Preparing for Court Appearances*
Theodore P. Remley, Jr., JD, PhD

Volume 2 *Documentation in Counseling Records*
Robert W. Mitchell, ACSW

Volume 3 *Law and Management of a Counseling Agency or Private Practice*
Ronald K. Bullis, MDiv, JD

Volume 4 *Counseling Minor Clients*
Mark M. Salo, MEd
Stephen G. Shumate, JD, MS

Volume 5 *The Counselor as Expert Witness*
William J. Weikel, PhD
Paula Richardson Hughes, JD

Volume 6 *Confidentiality and Privileged Communication*
Gibbs L. Arthur, Jr., MEd
Carl D. Swanson, JD, EdD

Volume 7 *Legal Issues in Marriage and Family Counseling*
Patricia Stevens-Smith, PhD
Marcia M. Hughes, JD

THE ACA LEGAL SERIES
Volume 4

"COUNSELING MINOR CLIENTS"

Mark M. Salo, MEd
Stephen G. Shumate, JD, MS

Series Editor
Theodore P. Remley, Jr., JD, PhD

AMERICAN COUNSELING ASSOCIATION

American Counseling Association
5999 Stevenson Avenue
Alexandria, VA 22304

Cover design by Sarah Jane Valdez

Library of Congress Cataloging-in-Publication Data

Salo, Mark M.
Counseling minor clients / Mark M. Salo, and Stephen G. Shumate
p. cm. — (ACA legal series, V. 4)
Includes bibliographical references.
ISBN 1-55620-103-6
1. Counseling—Law and legislation—United States. 2. Minors—United States. 3. Counselor and client. I. Shumate, Stephen G. II. Title. III. Series.
KF2900.S25 1993
347.73'03106—dc20
[347.3073106]

92-29704
CIP
ACA Legal Series Volume 4

Printed in the United States of America

To the memory of my father, Raymond J. Salo

To Jane

Contents

Contents

Biographies

Mark M. Salo is a middle school counselor for the Bozeman Public Schools in Bozeman, Montana. He holds an MEd in guidance and counseling from Montana State University where he regularly teaches counselor education courses. Mr. Salo chairs the American School Counselor Association Ethics Committee (1992–1993) and served as president of the Montana School Counselor Association in 1990–1991. He is a licensed professional counselor in Montana and is a National Certified Counselor.

Stephen G. Shumate holds an MS degree in counseling from North Dakota State University and a JD in law from the University of Montana. Mr. Shumate has served as a chemical dependency counselor, chemical dependency clinic director, university counselor educator, and consultant to counseling centers and school districts. He is currently a doctoral student in counselor education at the University of North Carolina–Greensboro.

Theodore P. Remley, Jr., Series Editor, is Executive Director of the American Counseling Association. Immediately prior to assuming this position, Dr. Remley was chair of the Department of Counselor Education at Mississippi State University in Starkville. He holds a PhD from the Department of Counselor Education at the University of Florida in Gainesville and a JD in law from the Catholic University of America in Washington, DC.

Preface

Counseling minor clients is an ambiguous practice. Legal and ethical uncertainties become daily stumbling blocks for professionals who work with minors. Can a child seek counseling services without a parent's knowledge? Do parents have the right to request access to counseling records regarding their son or daughter? When is counseling advice construed as unduly influencing an impressionable young mind?

There are no easy answers to these questions. This monograph is intended to be a guide for all counselors, social workers, psychologists, psychiatric nurses, and psychiatrists who work with children and adolescents across the United States. Finding absolute guidelines is difficult, particularly when state statutes and court decisions are far from being in agreement. What may hold true in one state may be entirely contrary across a state border. What may be a "best practice" in a private residential setting may be taboo in a public school. What may be a legal right for a 14-year-old may be out of the question for a youth of 13.

As a matter of general practice, children are treated differently than adults in the legal arena. This is deemed necessary to protect children from errors of judgment, particularly in criminal cases in which the minor has committed a crime. Society never permits a child of 8 to be tried as an adult in a homicide case. The legal system often insulates children from being held fully responsible for decisions taken before they have reached the age of reason. At the same time, the legal rights of minors can appear rather extensive, as in the case of a juvenile seeking medical treatment for a sexually transmitted disease without parental knowledge.

This monograph addresses many of the questions mental health professionals find themselves asking when faced with counseling minor clients. Pulling from their diverse backgrounds and professional experience in public education, private practice, and the legal sector, the authors have extensively researched the legal ramifications of providing counseling services for minor clients.

This monograph begins by examining how children and adolescents are viewed in the eyes of the law and discusses a minor's legal right to seek or refuse counseling services. Issues involving custody and competing interests for a child's welfare are addressed, as are special considerations for various work settings.

The ethical duties of confidentiality and the legal ramifications of privileged communication as they relate to minor clients are examined, as are exceptions to these practices, including the reporting of child abuse and assisting suicidal and homicidal youth. Other topics that are addressed include considerations for counseling minors about sexual activity and its consequences, dual relationship issues for counselors of children and adolescents, and federal statutes that delineate the responsibilities of counselors in handling educational records.

General answers to commonly asked questions provide practitioners with guidance, and specific guidelines for practice assist counselors in following best practices. A section containing discussion questions is included for university professors who want to use this monograph as a basis for instruction or for mental health professionals who are interested in further clarifying their personal knowledge.

As this monograph makes clear, the decision to enter into a counseling relationship with a minor client is not one to be made without carefully considering many factors, including the minor's age and maturity level, the work setting and its policies, parental consent for counseling (or the lack thereof), the minor's consent or resistance to counseling, the minor's intentions, the counselor's training and practice, and state and federal statutes applicable to the specific situation. In these stressful times, children and adolescents are in need of professional counseling services more than ever.

Throughout this monograph the authors strive to remain practical and understandable. This publication is intended to impart general ethical and legal knowledge and is not to be construed as providing legal advice. For specific concerns, counseling professionals are encouraged to consult attorneys familiar with the mental health field.

Glossary

Chattel: An article of personal property that is not real estate. In our not-so-distant past, children and slaves were considered chattel.

Child Enticement: An invitation or attempt to persuade a child to enter any vehicle, building, room, or secluded place with the intent to commit an unlawful sexual act upon or with the child.

Common Law: The body of those principles and rules of action that derive their authority from the judgments and decrees of courts, as distinguished from law created by legislatures.

Confidentiality: An ethical duty for all counselors and other mental health professionals not to reveal information related to them by clients. There are many exceptions to this responsibility for confidentiality.

Consent: The voluntary agreement by a person in the possession of and exercise of sufficient mental capacity to make an intelligent choice to do something proposed by another.

Contributing to the Delinquency of a Minor: Actions by an adult that encourage, facilitate, or otherwise directly support a minor's illegal acts or otherwise indecent or immoral conduct.

Custody of Children: The care, control, and maintenance of a child that may be awarded by a court to one of the parents in a divorce or separation proceeding.

Emancipated Minor: A minor who by court action is declared for most practical and legal purposes as having adult rights and responsibilities. Depending on specific state statutes, emancipation can occur through marriage, joining the armed services, or by the youth declaring economic independence from the parents.

Guardian Ad Litem: A special guardian appointed by the court who acts as an officer in the court representing solely the interest of a child or incompetent person in litigation. This person may or may not be an attorney.

Informed Forced Consent: The practice of informing a minor of why he or she is being seen in a counseling setting without being given the choice to refuse services. This is often the result of a parent's wish for the minor to receive counseling, as in the case of a residential treatment facility.

In Loco Parentis: A legal term describing a duty assigned to certain adults to act in place of a parent to a child in the parent's absence. This term is often used to describe the role of school personnel, although the depth of this authorization has been limited with more recent legal actions. In most states, a teacher does not have the right to use corporal punishment to discipline a child, whereas a parent retains this right within reasonable parameters.

Joint Custody of Children: A custody arrangement in which both parents retain equal legal right to the care, control, and maintenance of the child.

Jurisdiction: The geographic area and class of cases over which a court has power and authority to render legal decisions.

Majority (Age of Reason): The age at which, by law, a person is entitled to the management of his or her own affairs and to the enjoyment of civic rights.

Privileged Communication: In some instances, oral and written communications between specific professionals and their clients are categorized as privileged, and judges may not compel disclosure of the communications in a court of law. In order for a communication to be privileged, there must be a state statute that specifically identifies the communication between a category of professionals and their clients as privileged. The privilege belongs to clients, and they may waive their privilege if they wish.

Subpoena: A court document that orders a person to appear in court for a hearing or trial or at another location to be questioned regarding a pending lawsuit. Persons receiving a subpoena must comply unless the subpoena is withdrawn or is overruled by a judge. The penalty for noncompliance could include incarceration in jail or a fine.

Tort: A private or civil wrong or injury that results from violation of a duty owed from one party to another that does not arise from mere agreement of the parties.

Undue Influence: An improper or wrongful constraint, or urgency of persuasion, whereby the will of a person is overpowered, and he or she is induced to act contrary to the manner he or she would behave if left to act freely.

Vested: Given the rights of absolute ownership.

Child or Young Adult?

The legal status of children and adolescents presents a fascinating and often confusing challenge to the counselor. Despite the fact that minors possess a large measure of the same rights guaranteed to adults, parents and guardians often determine the assertion of a minor's rights. For a counselor, the dilemma of who retains the power to make decisions regarding counseling services begins at the first moment of contact with a parent or child seeking help.

In the early days of our country's history, there was little confusion about this issue. Until the age of majority, children were legally treated as chattel (property) of their parents. All decisions affecting the child were vested in these guardians. Despite significant erosion of this legal principle over time, a parent's legal ability to determine what activities a child may pursue remains strong, especially during the preteen years. Young children lack the capacity to understand fully the risks and benefits of important decisions. In 1979 the United States Supreme Court declared:

> We have recognized three reasons justifying the conclusion that the constitutional rights of children cannot be equated with those of adults: the peculiar vulnerability of children; their inability to make critical decisions in an informed,

mature manner; and the importance of the parental role in child rearing. (*Belotti v. Baird*, 1979)

Furthermore, the Court stated in 1981, "We have recognized that parents have an important 'guiding role' to play in the upbringing of their children which presumptively includes counseling them on important decisions" (*H.L. v. Matheson*, 1981).

Despite the apparent clarity of the Court's position on minors' rights, the murky waters of juvenile and tort law affect our ability as counselors to rely on clearly stated principles of legal policy. For example, despite the fact that minors generally cannot be bound by their contracts, they can be held liable for intentional and negligent injuries inflicted on others. Minors usually cannot marry without parental consent, but they have been found competent to waive their right to legal counsel. Most states have criminal cases on record in which a minor has been bound over to adult criminal court to be tried by standards applicable to adults.

When a child approaches a counselor without parental knowledge or consent, immediate tension arises between the child's right to privacy and the parent's right—on the child's behalf—to provide informed consent for the counseling. Generally, the younger the child, the more rights are vested in the parents. Once minors reach teenage years and display increasing capacity for rational decision making, both the common law and statutory law recognize this capacity by providing more legal autonomy for minors in carefully prescribed areas.

The exception to the common law doctrine requiring parental consent for the treatment of minors is the "mature minor rule" that allows an adolescent limited autonomous decision-making power usually related to medical and mental health matters. See, for example, *Younts v. St. Francis Hospital* (1970) and Wadlington (1973). Courts generally review several factors when reviewing a mature minor case. Among these are (1) whether the treatment was undertaken for the direct benefit of the minor rather than a third party; (2) the age of the minor (at least in the range of 14 on up); (3) the impracticability of obtaining parental consent; (4) the ability of the minor to appreciate the proposed intervention; and (5) whether the attention given was in response to an emergency, and whether nonemergency procedures were less than "major" or "serious" in nature (Wadlington, 1973). Recently, courts have extended this principle to include a mature minor's right to refuse lifesaving medical attention (*In re E.G.*, 1989).

Statutes in many states and certain federal regulations now permit unemancipated minors of sufficient maturity (usually between 14 and 16 years of age and on up) to make autonomous and crucial medical and mental health decisions. (See the representative listing of state statutes at the end of the References section, and see also the discussion of federal confidentiality laws related to alcohol and drug treatment in the Records chapter.) Legislators increasingly recognize that parental consent requirements often deter minors from seeking needed care for sexually transmitted disease, contraception, pregnancy, chemical dependency, and mental or emotional disorders. Public health policy concerns often outweigh parents' vested interests in providing consent for the minor (American Bar Association, 1980). These statutes vary widely from state to state. Some allow only limited care before a parent must be notified, and several delineate and limit who may provide service and for what reason. Again, counselors must become familiar with the specific law of their state and seek legal consultation when unclear situations arise.

In addition, common law and many state statutes recognize adolescent emancipation from parents if certain conditions are met. The legal doctrine of emancipation severs the parent's control over the child's rights. Conversely, it also ends the child's right to parental support. Although courts apply no hard or fast rule when determining emancipation, a rebuttable presumption against emancipation exists prior to attaining majority (*Niesen v. Niesen*, 1968; *Newburg v. Arrigo*, 1982). At common law, emancipation usually requires the consent, expressed or implied, of the parent. However, parental abandonment, abuse, or neglect are often sufficient grounds for findings of emancipation. Courts also have granted emancipation upon marriage or entry into the armed forces. Emancipation may be temporary or permanent, total or partial, and generally does not grant the right to consume alcohol, vote, or enter binding contracts. One of the major criteria for granting emancipation concerns the youth's financial ability to provide for himself or herself. As a result, most emancipation statutes limit petitions to minors age 16 and older, the age when youths can seek gainful employment and drive automobiles.

State laws vary widely regarding emancipation. As with all legal matters, it is crucial to check specific emancipation statutes in one's local jurisdiction.

Another confusing issue for counselors concerns whether a minor has the legal right to refuse counseling that parents deem essential. Although many counselors terminate or refer children who display consistent resistance, there are occasions when parents seek to abdicate their responsibilities as parents by repeatedly forcing children into counseling and imposing a "problem child" identity upon them. Unfortunately, a child may have no legal recourse. In rare cases when parental coercion is severe, a counselor may decide to report the abuse to family protection services. Most of the time several simple interventions with the family will suffice (Schutz, 1986).

Another common problem concerns the child who seeks counseling help, often in a school setting, against his or her parents' wishes. Unless one of the legal exceptions noted previously is present, the parents will probably succeed in a legal attempt (an injunction) to bar the counseling. This is especially true if the child is under 14 years of age.

Finally, the most common instance concerns a child seeking counseling without the knowledge and consent of a parent. At common law, counselors generally are under no affirmative duty to inform or obtain parental consent for the counseling of children unless the child lacks the capacity to make an informed decision regarding counseling services. State statutes and employment policies and procedures may be more specific regarding age limitations and capacity to consent to counseling. Counselors should be aware of their state's statutes and case law in this area; ignorance of the law is no defense. However, it is also important to note that successful injury suits against counselors for counseling minors generally have been limited to egregious malpractice actions and cases of shocking or outrageous conduct intended to harm the child or family. Cases of this nature are quite rare. The greatest legal protection for the counselor is the fact that ethical counseling rarely injures or causes monetary damage. In their research, Croxton, Churchill, and Fellin (1988) failed to find a single instance in which a mental health professional was sued for either child enticement or any similar action resulting from counseling minors without parental permission—despite the large increase in services being provided for children and adolescents in the last 20 years.

Remote liability, however, does little to resolve the ethical and clinical dilemmas when a counselor must decide whether to work with a minor without parental knowledge or consent. Most clinicians agree that in the absence of foreseeable harm to the minor, parents should be informed of the minor's decision to initiate counseling. Early communication and agreement regarding the purpose of counseling and the limits of confidentiality can prevent problems later. Parents can be valuable allies in the counseling process. In most cases, they deserve the opportunity to enhance their positive influence.

Divided Loyalties

Counselors who provide services for children and adolescents regularly find themselves caught in the middle of competition among conflicting adult desires for that child. Disagreements frequently occur among custodial parents, noncustodial parents, stepparents, foster parents, religious authorities, childcare caseworkers, teachers, other mental health professionals, and guardian ad litem attorneys. It is not uncommon to receive a plethora of conflicting professional and lay direction for what help, if any, the child requires.

This problem is particularly acute during impending divorce when a custody dispute arises. The courts generally apply the legal doctrine known as *best interests of the child* in determining which parent receives custody and what visitation rights the noncustodial parent retains. Best interests of the child include, but are not limited to, the following criteria (Horowitz & Davidson, 1984; Meyer, Landis, & Hays, 1988):

- the love, affection, and other emotional ties existing between the competing parties and the child
- the capacity and disposition of competing parties to give the child love, affection, and guidance, and to continue the educating and raising of the child in his or her religion or creed, if any

- the capacity and disposition of competing parties to provide the child with shelter, food, clothing, medical care, and other necessities
- the length of time the child has lived in a stable, satisfactory environment and the desirability of maintaining continuity
- the permanence, as a family unit, of the existing or proposed custodial home
- the moral fitness of the competing parties
- the home, school, and community record of the child
- the mental and physical health of the competing parties
- the reasonable preference of the child, if the court deems the child to be of sufficient age to express this preference. The preferences of preteens have significantly diminished influence on the court

Most counselors are reluctant to get involved in custody matters; nevertheless, marital discord and divorce create great stress in a family, and children commonly react with acting out and other dysfunctional behavior. Often counselors begin seeing a child before separation or divorce occurs only to find themselves weeks later embroiled in a custody dispute or postdivorce contest among other interested parties.

Counselors usually can maintain perspective and rise above the fray by following a few simple principles:

1. Remember that the legal rights of a minor reside in the custodial parent or guardian. Noncustodial parents, stepparents, other family members, and interested parties must defer to the decisions of the custodial parent unless there is a court order to the contrary. A counselor must know with certainty who retains legal custody of the child. He or she should ask for written proof and not accept verbal assurances.
2. Signed informed consent from the custodial parent or guardian should be obtained for the counseling services provided. This may also be a good idea for school counselors who normally do not require parental consent.
3. Impeccable records should be kept with clear divisions between objective and subjective content, in the very real possibility that records may be subpoenaed and end up in court.
4. A client's confidentiality should be carefully guarded. Releases of information should be signed by both the custodial parent

and the minor if he or she understands consent. In many jurisdictions, noncustodial parents have access to a minor's school and medical records. Some jurisdictions allow record exchanges between health care providers without releases of information, provided the client is being treated concurrently by both providers. When in doubt, legal advice should be sought before responding to an inquiry.

With the increased prevalence of joint custody decrees during the past 20 years, counselors increasingly find themselves caught between a custodial parent who wants the child to obtain counseling and another custodial parent who refuses counseling for the child. Unfortunately, no standard response fits this difficult situation. Counselors often must exercise their own best-interests-of-the-child test in deciding a course of action, especially when one or both parents directly pressure the child to act in violation of the opposing parent's wishes. When possible, the counselor can attempt to mediate the dispute by meeting with both parents. Sometimes assisting the parents in receiving outside mediation is helpful. Some counselors schedule sessions only when the consenting parent has physical custody of the child. This places the burden on the nonconsenting parent to seek a legal hearing and court decree deciding the matter for all parties concerned. Unfortunately, cessation of counseling may be the wisest option of all because continued counseling under coerced or adverse conditions may provide limited benefits for the child.

Many counselors are not aware that noncustodial parents retain the right to inspect and review the records of their children. In this regard, noncustodial parents have the same rights as custodial parents unless access has been prohibited by a court order. Most problems in this area can be prevented by taking a comprehensive family history during the initial interview and thoroughly ascertaining the custodial provisions for the child.

Setting Considerations

The decision to counsel a minor client—assuming the counselor has adequate training and experience with this age group—depends a great deal on the work setting, any applicable state statutes, the minor's age and maturity level, and whether or not parental consent has been obtained. It is the setting in which a counselor is employed that often dictates how a minor client is provided services, or even whether a counseling relationship is established at all. A middle school counselor, for example, is likely to approach a request for counseling differently than a counselor in private practice.

Because policies and practices vary widely from setting to setting, differences in the roles of school, agency, and private practice counselors are many. Each setting—school, agency, and private practice—warrants a closer examination.

1. School Settings

Because minors are counseled most often in schools, the school counselor, more than counselors in other settings, is most often faced with conflicts about minors (Hummel, Talbutt, & Alexander 1985). In an unsuccessful suit brought by parents against a school counselor in Pennsylvania for a multitude of alleged violations, a U.S. federal district court noted that "the constitutional rights of children, parents, administrators, and teachers are all competing in the schools. But these rights are not absolute and must be balanced against the rights of other individuals and also the rights of the state" (*Roman v. Appleby*, 1983).

School counseling primarily emerged from society's perceived need to provide youth with career guidance in America's high schools in the immediate post-Sputnik period. From there, it was a natural step for school "guidance" personnel to begin providing personal and emotional counseling as the needs for additional services became more apparent, first in the high schools, then in the middle and junior high schools, and most recently at the elementary levels. Graduate-level training programs for school counselors have responded to the changes, with many individuals now being nationally certified and state licensed in addition to holding state counselor certification. School counselors now work with individuals, groups, and families, and provide broad services across the entire range of issues, from career counseling to child abuse. A minor's initiation to mental health therapy often begins with a school counselor's intervention.

Generally, school counselors provide services to individual or groups of students when the educational process of learning is interrupted by social, emotional, or academic concerns. Although a school counselor may have received master's-level training in the "deeper" therapeutic methods, his or her practice is often limited to short-term interventions and relatively minor adjustment issues. This is also a necessity when counselors are staffed at a student-to-counselor ratio of 400 (or more!) to 1. Students in need of long-term therapy for deeply seated emotional concerns are usually referred to community resources. School counselors may also "educate" the general school population through preventive classroom guidance activities covering such areas as communication, problem solving, and decision making. Many school counselors are also responsible for class scheduling, student records, and career counseling and must serve as key members of various teams designed to meet individual student needs. Teachers, administrators, students, and parents all place demands upon the school counselor. Sometimes these requests for services are in conflict with each other, and it is the counselor's responsibility to weigh the many factors involved.

Historically, the school counselor is seen as a part of the general school support staff, much like a school nurse, and so access to counseling personnel is seen as a service available to the entire school population. The authors are not aware of any state or federal statutes requiring school counselors to obtain parent permission to counsel minors of any age, although some schools and districts have adopted policies requiring that permission be obtained before counseling services are provided, most frequently in the elementary grade levels, sometimes after an initial visit or two. This practice is in contrast to federal guidelines that require parent permission for psychological testing for children being evaluated for eligibility for special education services.

School counselors receive many referrals from parents to counsel their children. Often the child is in agreement, or at least neutral, regarding the request for services, but occasionally they are outright resistant. Although it is important for a school counselor to attempt to work carefully through a child's resistance, pushing the student against his or her will probably creates more harm than benefit. Schools are not residential treatment facilities, and a student's personal comfort is important, as is the counselor's reputation with the student body. When a student continues to resist counseling, it is wise for the counselor to inform the parent that he or she is unable to be effective and to offer possible alternatives or referrals.

Recording personal counseling notes on each student contact during a typically hectic day could be extremely time consuming for a school counselor. A fair number of routine matters that are handled in routine ways (schedule changes or requests for information, for example) never require documentation, but it is a good idea to keep brief case notes on students that are seen on a regular basis, or if the situation has a potential for going to court, as in custody battles or abuse cases. Any written note can be subpoenaed in a court of law, so it is best to avoid making highly speculative or defamatory comments. Remember to keep counseling notes in a secure place, away from a student's regular cumulative file.

School counselors often refer students or their families to outside agencies or private practitioners. Normally the receiving professional(s) requests that the school counselor release information contained in his or her personal counseling notes. If the release of information form has been signed by the parent, the counselor should comply. It is also ethically responsible to at-

Agency counselors, like school counselors, should always follow orders of supervisors unless a counselor is directed to do something that is illegal, clearly unethical, or in violation of an institutional policy or procedure (Remley, 1990). Insubordination is grounds for dismissal. An order may, however, be protested to the supervisor's supervisor if it is felt that it is unfair or inappropriate.

One specific area of concern for agency counselors in working with minors is the idea of "informed forced consent," which is when parents impose counseling upon their offspring. In residential treatment facilities that operate under a medical model, children and adolescents are often seen as patients and committed to a therapeutic program, often against their will. Ask most adolescent newcomers to a chemical abuse treatment center if they would stay in the program if they had the choice, and the answer is sure to be a resounding "No!" Involuntary commitment is recognized as a legal necessity virtually everywhere, although conditions vary widely from state to state. Generally, a person can be declared incapable of making his or her own decisions for a variety of emotional or chemical concerns. This is especially true of minors who are deemed to have limited decision-making skills. In these circumstances, the parent is exerting his or her right to state what is best for the child, and as has been noted, the Supreme Court is firmly behind the concept of the parent knowing what is best for his or her children.

3. Private Practice Settings

Private practice counselors are small business owners, co-owners, or employees of larger firms. As such, their practice is often based on an hourly fee structure for services delivered. Private counselors usually hold master's degrees or doctorates in counseling and therapy, are licensed or certified in most states, and frequently offer services in specialized areas of interest and training such as eating disorders, addictions, or marriage and family therapy. The private practitioner is often responsible for every aspect of the business, including marketing and promotional work, client intake and therapy, and fee collection and insurance company billing.

Many private practitioners with proper training and experience accept children and adolescents as clients, either individually or in conjunction with their parents. If prospective clients are required to read and sign an agreement at the outset of counseling, is it legally binding if the client is a minor? The answer revolves around "informed consent" and the youth's ability to comprehend the conditions of the agreement. Are there any state statutes that can guide the counselor? In Alabama, for example, any minor who is 14 years of age or older may give sole consent for any legally authorized medical or mental health service for himself or herself (*Alabama Code Ann.*, 1984). Generally, minors cannot be held to a contract that they sign because the law sees them as lacking the maturity to judge the ramifications of the conditions of the agreement (consent). Of course, if a parent is willing to cosign a services agreement, then the parent is obligated to see that a counselor is reimbursed for his or her services.

If clients are reimbursed by health insurance companies for counseling services, the counselor is obligated to meet insurance company procedures. Normally children are covered under their parents' or guardians' personal or group health insurance plan, which means that parental cooperation is crucial. Specific limitations of an insurance policy should be noted. Clients are sometimes limited in the number of visitations allowed, fees charged, or the total amount permitted to be billed within a certain period of time. Also, mental health services may not be covered under various health insurance policies.

Liability insurance is a must for private practitioners, who cannot rely on a supervisor or an agency to insulate them from lawsuits. In today's litigious society anyone can be sued for any imagined harm, although the lawsuits brought against counselors are relatively few in number and usually involve gross misconduct. Liability insurance is a "license to relax" (Remley, 1990).

Confidentiality and Privileged Communication

Perhaps the most difficult area of concern facing counselors of minor clients is that of confidentiality. Graduate schools and ethical standards emphasize developing and maintaining confidential relationships in order to provide a solid base of trust and encourage sharing of intimate thoughts. Most mental professionals and their clients deem the privacy of the counseling relationship a necessity. Thus requests for information are of great concern, particularly, for example, a parent's request for information about counseling sessions with his or her child—when that parent is paying the bill.

Confusion exists in the mental health profession about the definitions of *confidentiality* and *privileged communication*. Although the two terms are sometimes used interchangeably, their legal implications are distinct. *Confidentiality* is considered an ethical or moral term describing a decision not to reveal the contents of information gained in the counseling relationship. Statutory laws often do not specifically protect counselor-client confidentiality in court proceedings, but the standard of care for most counseling contexts recognizes confidentiality as essential to the counseling process. Unwarranted violations of confidentiality can be cause for a malpractice action against the counselor. Counselors always have an ethical obligation to maintain a client's confidentiality. Children have a moral right to their privacy, and the ethical counselor supports this to the extent possible.

Privileged communication, however, is a legal concept. States have adopted various statutes that grant privilege to relationships between citizens and specific professionals. Communications resulting from these relationships are granted the "privilege" of being exempt from court orders that they be disclosed. Historically, the lawyer-client and husband-wife relationships are the only ones deemed sacred enough to be considered privileged. Privileged communication rights have gradually been extended to include doctor-patient, priest-parishioner, and counselor-client relationships, although there is a tremendous variation among the 50 states.

In privileged communication statutes, it is generally agreed that the specific mental health provider must be indicated. For example, if a privileged communication statute is written for licensed psychologists and licensed professional counselors, the privilege does not extend to school counselors unless the school counselor also happens to be a licensed psychologist or licensed professional counselor.

It should be noted that the decision to reveal information covered under privileged communication statutes is the client's, not the counselor's, and stems from the Fifth Amendment right to privacy. If a client requests that a counselor reveal information, he or she is obligated to do so.

Privacy rights for minors are generally seen as an extension of the parents' rights to privacy; minors do not hold these rights in isolation from their parents. The Family Educational Rights and Privacy Act of 1974 (also know as FERPA or the Buckley Amendment) clearly articulates that schools receiving federal funding may not disclose a child's educational record without the consent of parents or guardians and that students may not exercise this right of consent until they have reached the age of 18. The extension of privacy rights to minor clients is nebulous. As Croxton, Churchill, and Fellin (1988) observed, ". . . the United States Supreme Court has yet to develop a clearly articulated policy delineating where the privacy rights of minors end and the rights of parents begin" (p. 4). The courts continue to see parents as being primarily responsible for the upbringing of their children, and counselors do have legal obligations to the parents or guardians of the children they counsel. The U.S. Supreme Court has affirmed parents' rights to have a primary "guiding role" to play in the upbringing of their children (*H.L. v. Matheson*, 1981). Minors lack the capacity to make fully informed, voluntary decisions in the eyes of the law.

One particular issue involves children requesting counseling services in direct opposition to parental wishes. If a parent insists that a counselor not see his or her child, even if the child continues to seek counseling services, it is wise to follow the parent's wishes. One approach is to document the concerns and recommendations, turn the matter over to a supervisor or the local child protective service agency, and let go. The counselor invites trouble by countermanding a direct parental order not to counsel a child (Salo & Shumate, 1991).

1. Handling Requests for Information

The question of whether to divulge information gained through a counseling relationship with a minor to requesting adults is a difficult one. Often counselors feel it necessary to share information with significant adults to assist the counseling process. In addition, school counselors are often pried for information about specific children by teachers and administrators. Sheeley and Herlihy (1987) noted that:

> In working with clients who are minors, school counselors must frequently involve adults for counseling to be effective. As a result, the pupil's right to confidentiality is sometimes outweighed by the need to inform parents, guardians, teachers, or other adults. (p. 271)

Prior to sharing information gained in counseling sessions, the counselor should consider several factors, including who has requested the information, whether the parent or guardian has given permission to disclose, and whether the minor has been consulted about the disclosure.

If the requesting person is a parent or guardian of the client, he or she probably has a legal right to know the content of counseling sessions (Remley, 1990). This follows logically on the basis that privacy rights belong to the parent, even if the child or adolescent does not wish the information be divulged. This also runs contrary to the sanctity of the counseling relationship as generally taught in graduate school and published in professional ethical codes. Ethical standards do not supersede the law, and obtaining minor consent prior to divulging information is an ethical issue only. If the requesting person is a third party, the law requires parent permission before disclosure is made. In schools, this legal tenet may be compromised when counselors share confidential information with teachers and other staff members. Only staff members with an "educational need to know" should be given information, however. A prudent practice is to have the child and parent sign a release before disclosing any information.

If a counselor has reservations about revealing information he or she feels is ethically confidential, the outcome of such a request depends, to a large degree, on how the counselor frames the response to the requesting adult. Remley (1990) suggested five possible ways to handle these requests:

- Try to persuade the adult that the child's best interests are not served by revealing the information. Attempt to educate the inquiring adult about the nature of the counseling relationship.
- Discuss the inquiry with the minor and see if he or she is willing to disclose the content of the counseling session to the adult. Sometimes counselors are more concerned than a child about his or her privacy.
- Schedule a joint session with the adult and the minor. Hope that the adult will change his or her mind about wanting the information or that the minor will be willing to disclose enough information to satisfy the adult.
- Inform the child ahead of time and then disclose the content of the session to the inquiring adult. If the adult is not a parent or guardian, inform the parent or guardian before disclosing the information.
- Refuse to disclose the information to the inquiring adult (and assume the resulting liabilities).

A difficult issue arises when a noncustodial parent requests information concerning his or her child's disclosures to a counselor about the child's relationship with the custodial parent. In this circumstance, the counselor is wise to obtain permission from the custodial parent before revealing any information. If this is not possible, the court has to decide the issue since both parents have equal legal rights unless there is a specific court ruling to the contrary.

2. The "Duty to Warn" Exception

Most mental health professionals recognize the necessity of compromising confidentiality when faced with situations in which either the client or another is in danger, or when there is a legal requirement to testify in a court of law. Suicide threats or threats of harm to specific individuals are instances in which confidentiality responsibilities are secondary to an obligation to prevent harm. Counselors can be found liable for malpractice for failing to take appropriate action to prevent harm.

The now familiar *Tarasoff* decision by the California Supreme Court found that psychotherapists in California are responsible for warning an intended victim directly if that person's identity is known (*Tarasoff v. Regents of the State of California*, 1976). Although this case involved a college student who committed murder after revealing his intentions to his psychotherapist, the implications for counselors of minor clients are clear. If a minor client reveals deadly intentions toward a known victim, the counselor must take proper action. A warning to the authorities is sometimes appropriate, but may not be sufficient in itself to satisfy the legal obligations in a specific state's "duty to warn" statute.

To take reasonable precautions, the parents of a minor making threats should be informed, as should the intended victim and his or her parents. This point is illustrated in the case of *McIntosh v. Milano* (1979), in which an adolescent boy in New Jersey was referred to a psychiatrist by a school counselor. In later counseling sessions the boy spoke of harmful intentions toward a girl who lived next door. Although the therapist talked with the boy's parents, neither the girl nor her parents were ever contacted. The girl was then murdered by the boy. The superior court of New Jersey ruled that the therapist "may have a duty to take whatever steps are reasonably necessary to protect an intended or potential victim." The court went on to state that a "practitioner may have to protect the welfare of the community." The intended victim's need to know (and his or her parents' need to know, if the intended victim is a minor) clearly supersedes the client's right to confidentiality or privileged communication.

Court decisions have continued to push the counselor's legal obligations to protect individuals, and society in general, from potentially violent clients. Counselors may have to move beyond the step of warning others to taking whatever means are justified in a situation, including attempting in some way to detain the client. In any malpractice suit brought against a counselor, a court is sure to look at the professional's actions to determine if reasonable and prudent attempts were made to prevent the violence from occuring.

Counselors may also have a duty to warn any person or group of danger presented by a client. In Vermont a court found a counselor partially negligent in a lawsuit for not warning a couple that their son, a client, had threatened to burn their barn (*Peck v. Counseling Service of Addison County, Inc.*, 1985). The court saw arson as a violent act involving a threat to humans and ruled that the counselor had a duty to warn the parents of such a threat.

When informing others of potentially harmful conditions, the counselor is urged to violate confidentiality to the minimum degree possible (Remley, 1990). It is also a wise practice to explain exceptions to confidentiality prior to beginning a professional relationship in both verbal and written form.

3. The Child Abuse Reporting Exception

Another major exception to confidentiality concerns a counselor's duty to report confirmed or suspected child abuse or neglect. Most states have specific statutes delineating reporting requirements and procedures. It is important for a counselor to know and understand the exact wording in his or her state's statutes.

Deciding to report child abuse is fairly straightforward when a child has readily identifiable injuries obviously resulting from an adult's violent actions. Most counselors do not hesitate when faced with evidence that intervention is required to protect a child from further harm. Counselors must also report suspected cases of child abuse or neglect, and in fact, they are obligated to act to protect children from the possibilities of future injury.

Although this type of reporting is subjective and the potential for error is always present, the laws of all states authorize child protective service agencies and courts to intervene before children have suffered an injury, even a minor one (Besharov, 1988). Counselors making a report of known or suspected abuse in any state are functioning under their statutory duty as professionals, and so long as the counselor is acting without malicious intent toward the suspected abusive adult, he or she is immune from liability for making a report that turns out to be without merit upon investigation by the proper authorities (Cambin & Prout, 1983).

Several legal cases have made it clear that a professional's failure to report child abuse is a negligent action. The Supreme Court of California ruled in 1976 that a physician and hospital could be held liable for a child's injuries if they "negligently failed to diagnose and report battered child syndrome, resulting in the child's being returned to her parents and receiving further injuries at their hands" (*Landeros v. Flood*, 1976). Another case involving a psychiatrist's failure to report abuse brought the issue of nonreporting to the mental health profession: In *Groff v. State of Florida* (1980), a Florida court of appeals found that "Dr. Groff was subject to penalty for failure to report child abuse. . . ." Although these cases involved medically trained individuals, counselors and other mental health professionals may also be held to expected standards of care relevant to the profession. With the recent increase in professional credentialing comes a more clearly defined obligation to report suspected child abuse.

Counselors and other professionals are often required to file a report of known or suspected child abuse with a specific child protective agency; notifying a supervisor may not satisfy the counselor's statutory duty. For example, section 41-3-201 of the Montana Codes Annotated (1991) states, "When the professionals and officials listed . . . know or have reasonable cause to suspect, as a result of information they receive in their professional or official capacity, that a child is abused or neglected, they shall report the matter promptly to the department of family services or its local affiliate. . . ." Any Montana school district or agency that has a policy requiring a counselor to report child abuse solely to a supervisor or review team is not conforming to the state statute and may leave the counselor open to claims of negligence.

Before making a report, it is ethically responsible for the counselor to notify the child of his or her intent to release the information. It is also appropriate to obtain the parent's release if he or she is not involved in the suspected abuse, although the law makes it mandatory to report, with or without parent permission.

Keeping adequate records in suspected child abuse situations is extremely important in the event the case goes to court. Counselors are often subpoenaed to testify in such circumstances, and documented records are necessary to establish professional credibility and give accurate testimony.

4. Other Exceptions

Several other exceptions to confidentiality and privileged communication exist: If judges order counselors to release information, they can reasonably state their objections; but they will be required to turn over counseling records, written or otherwise, or they may be found in contempt of court. Counselors should consult with an attorney if they feel their rights as professionals are being abused. Legal consultation is considered an ethical practice.

Although counselors may legally use a clerical assistant to process case notes, the supervising counselor is responsible for assuring that the secretary does not violate the client's right to privacy. Under no circumstance should minor office workers (student office aides, for example) have access to counseling case notes or other sensitive files. Adult secretaries should be educated about the sensitive nature of the material involved.

5. Group Counseling: A Unique Problem

Group counseling poses a unique problem for the counselor. Counselors must ethically do their best to keep the contents of group sessions confidential, but it has become a general tenet of law that having a third party present negates the privileged communication status of that conversation (*Perira v. U.S.*, 1974). Groups, by their very nature, negate the presumption of privacy. This also holds true when a minor client has a third party present for "moral support." A counselor could be obligated to testify in a court of law—even in states specifically granting privileged communication—by the fact that another party was present in the room. The counselor has a responsibility to inform all group participants of the need for confidentiality and the absence of legal privilege concerning group discussions (Hopkins & Anderson, 1990).

Additionally, counselors have no control over other group members' violations of confidentiality. Noncounselors do not have legal or ethical obligations to keep information discussed in groups in confidence. The use of confidentiality agreements, signed by group members or their parents, are not valid in court, and group members can be required to testify regarding other group members if the presiding judge orders it.

When counseling minor clients, the ethical mental health professional respects their confidentiality to the extent possible in a given situation. A minor's rights to privacy and privileged communication, if granted by specific state statute, are, however, vested in his or her parents or legal guardians, and counselors may be legally obligated to disclose information at the parents' or guardians' request. Consulting with other professionals in uncertain situations is always a positive practice.

Sexual Activity and Its Consequences

A minor's emerging sexual maturity is a potent and often divisive issue in intrafamily relations. Aside from far-reaching physical consequences, the onset of sexual activity marks another major step in the transition from child to adult. Intimate contact with someone outside the nuclear family generates varying degrees of difficulty as parents adjust to what may feel like an invasion of family privacy. Extrafamilial involvements also signal the approaching emancipation and independence of the minor.

Adolescent sexual activity brings myriad potential problems to a minor's life. Contemporary journalism reflects the reality that adolescents are sexually active at ever earlier ages, teenage pregnancy is epidemic, the prevalence of sexually transmitted disease (including AIDS) is increasing among our youth, and the rate of abortion among minors is rising. As critical decisions regarding sexual activity and its consequences are made, counselors working with minors face difficult issues concerning their ethical and legal duties to both the child and parent. Often minors resist disclosure to parents of their sexual activity or sexually related medical needs for fear of reprisal or simply out of embarrassment and shame. Professionals working with youth and their sexual-medical needs recognize that privacy and confidentiality are essential if adolescents are voluntarily to seek help with these delicate health issues. The U.S. Supreme Court also recognized a minor's need for privacy when in *Carey v. Population Servs. Int'l.* (1977) it held that "The right to privacy in connection with decisions affecting procreation extends to minors as well as adults." Fortunately, many state legislatures also have responded to the overriding importance of a minor's access to sexual-medical treatment and counseling at the minor's independent instigation and without stringent requirements for parental consent or notification. (A representative sample of state laws is included at the end of the References section.) These laws vary widely among the states, and counselors must become familiar with the particular statutes applicable in their jurisdiction and their attendant duties, limits, and immunities governing professional conduct.

Few issues today generate as much controversy as a woman's decision regarding pregnancy and abortion. When the woman is actually a young girl and the father a young boy, all concerned parties agonize over questions of health, morality, and the futures of these young people. Answers don't come easily, and regardless of the decision reached, some suffering seems inevitable. Much of the controversy finds its way to the legal arena. After years of relative legislative and judicial calm regarding the right to abortion, the issue once again occupies the forefront of political, legislative, and judicial attention.

In the landmark *Roe v. Wade* (1973) decision, the U.S. Supreme Court held that the due process clause of the 14th Amendment to the U.S. Constitution forbids states from interfering with a woman's choice to terminate her pregnancy. However, the Court also stated that a woman's fundamental right "is not unqualified and must be considered against important state interests in abortion." With a "compelling state interest" and "narrowly drawn" legislation, state regulation of abortion is permissible (*Roe v. Wade*, 1973).

The U.S. Supreme Court also has held that the states have a "significant interest in supporting certain abortion regulations aimed at protecting children which is not present in the case of an adult." As a result the Court has recognized that states have a significant interest in promoting parental consultation with a minor before she elects abortion. However, the Court also has held that states do not have the authority "to give a third party an absolute, a possibly arbitrary, veto" over the minor's abortion decision. Several states have responded by developing judicial bypass procedures in an effort to retain their parental notification requirement. The bypass allows the child to petition the court and demonstrate that she is mature enough to make a decision that an abortion is in her best interest or, even if she is not mature enough, that an abortion remains her best option. The judicial bypass procedure must not unduly burden the minor's right to an abortion. Therefore most of the controversy surrounding the bypass procedure concerns the length of waiting periods. Presently over 20 states require parental consent before a minor can have an abortion. At least 13 states require notification of one or both parents. Several of these state statutes are being challenged under court injunctions or other litigation and therefore have not yet been enforced (National Abortion Federation, 1991).

Constitutional challenges of spouse or father notification statutes turn on the issue of whether the law places an obstacle in the path of a woman's free exercise of her abortion decision. The U.S. Supreme Court has spoken once on the issue, and numerous federal courts have entertained challenges to these notification statutes. To date no father or spousal notification statute has been upheld.

Abortion law changes rapidly. With the U.S. Supreme Court's 1989 *Webster* decision, states now have increased flexibility to enact restrictions on abortion. The landmark case decided by the Court in 1992, *Planned Parenthood of Southeastern Pennsylvania v. Casey*, upheld provisions of a Pennsylvania law that required a woman under age 18 to secure permission from one of her parents or seek permission from a judge before obtaining an abortion. The decision also confirms a state's right to impose a 24-hour waiting period and to require doctors to inform women about other options. A provision requiring a woman to notify her husband (and probably any father) of an abortion was struck down.

A pregnant minor who seeks counseling usually knows little or nothing about parental notification or consent laws, and often has not considered the full impacts and requirements of carrying a child to term or raising a child herself. She will need to be educated about these matters and the requirements of the law, and assisted in considering her options. Skilled counselors must not only have a working familiarity with state law but must also recognize their professional limitations. Proper and timely referrals to appropriate legal and medical service providers are essential. Adoption counseling may become necessary. The school system and child care resources are crucial if the mother chooses to keep the child. Financial support from the father and his family may need to be established. The list of potential issues seems endless. Counselors necessarily must become adept at drawing upon and coordinating with a variety of service providers while maintaining the focus and scope of their particular counseling expertise.

Finally, a number of contemporary issues now emerge that pose interesting legal and ethical dilemmas for counselors. Does an HIV-positive minor present a "danger to self or others" if that minor continues sexual activity? Does the counselor have a duty to warn identifiable and intended sexual partners of this HIV-positive minor? If a minor has other serious sexually transmitted diseases, do the same rules apply? Does a legal duty arise from the counselor to the parents in these cases? No hard and fast law applies to many emerging counseling dilemmas. As with many counseling issues that arise in the course of working with minors, counselors must exercise the highest professional judgment, seek appropriate consultation when necessary, and support the integrity of the minor's family whenever possible.

Dual Relationships

The act of counseling children and adolescents carries an awesome ethical responsibility. Young people look to adults as models on which to base their future adult thoughts and behaviors, yet counselors are obligated by ethical standards not to interject their own values and decisions. "Impressionable young minds" are often open to adult input, especially after the establishment of a trusting counseling relationship. Parents entrust to counselors the emotional development of their offspring. A mental health professional should not underestimate the power of his or her persuasion, unintentional though it may be.

The possibility of either intentional or unintentional misuse of a counselor's influence is perhaps most clearly seen when a dual relationship develops between a counselor and a minor client. Dual relationships occur when professionals assume two roles simultaneously or sequentially with a person seeking help (Herlihy & Corey, 1992). Both roles may be professional, as in being a youth's teacher and his or her counselor, or the roles may be a combination of professional and nonprofessional, as in being a minor's counselor and little league coach. In any case, the counselor needs to maintain clarity and objectivity. Sometimes, the counseling relationship should be ethically terminated.

The *Ethical Standards* (AACD, 1988) state the following regarding dual relationships:

> When the member has other relationships, particularly of an administrative, and/or evaluative nature with an individual seeking counseling services, the member must not serve as the counselor but should refer the individual to another professional. Only in instances where such an alternative is unavailable and where the individual's condition warrants counseling intervention should the member enter into and/or maintain a counseling relationship. Dual relationships with clients that might impair the member's objectivity and professional judgment (e.g., as with close friends or relatives) must be avoided and/or the counseling relationship terminated through referral to another competent professional.

The dual relationship question broadens when we examine the wide range of possible dual relationships that can arise when counseling minor clients:

- A socially inept youth hugs the counselor and states "You're the best friend I ever had!"
- A school counselor is assigned to supervise the cafeteria during lunch time. Many of the students are the counselor's clients.
- A 16-year-old client ends up on the counselor's doorstep at 2 a.m. claiming to have been "kicked out of the house" by the client's stepfather.
- A counselor is attracted to a former client who is no longer a minor.
- The counselor of an adolescent is approached by the client's single parent for a date.
- A counselor is asked by a parent to counsel his or her son or daughter to "set them straight" about sexuality. The counselor believes homosexuality is a personal matter.
- A 14-year-old client presents the counselor with a gift certificate worth $10.00.

Obviously there are few absolute answers to questions related to these situations. It is an oversimplification to state that dual relationships must be avoided completely, although most ethical codes caution the practitioner to be wary. Sometimes there are no other professionals to refer a client to, as in a rural school setting with one counselor. At other times, serendipitous circumstances may create a dual relationship, as in a youth being placed on his counselor's summer soccer team. When a counselor becomes aware of the existence of a dual relationship, he or she should carefully weigh the possible benefits to the client against the possible harm stemming from the relationship. Dual role relationships challenge the counselor to monitor himself or herself and to examine the personal motivations for his or her practices (Herlihy & Corey, 1992).

It is natural for a counselor to establish friendships with the children he or she works with, but it is important that a professional distance be maintained in those relationships. A counselor cannot be a literal friend to an 8-year-old client, although the counselor might describe his or her role to the boy or girl as being supportive, accepting, and encouraging, which are certainly qualities of a good friend. In *The MasterTeacher* (1991), Robert DeBruyn discusses a "line" between being an adult friend and advocate to a student and being a buddy who acts more like a student than a professional. He notes that "If we think it's necessary to be a buddy to relate to students, we're wrong."

It is interesting to note that a legal doctrine, in loco parentis, is said to be in effect while children are in school. Effectively, this means that the teacher, principal, or counselor becomes the acting parent in the parent's absence, a dual relationship established by law. Although this concept has diminished considerably in recent years (Hummel, Talbutt, & Alexander, 1985), school counselors occasionally find themselves, either wittingly or unwittingly, in a parent substitute or authoritative role. An example of this occurs when school counselors are assigned to supervise students in study hall, on bus duty, or in the cafeteria. Counselors should be extremely cautious of personal motives and the potential for harming clients and counseling relationships whenever they become aware of the existence of a dual relationship. In this circumstance, counselors should work at educating the administration of the necessity to be excluded from direct student supervisory duties.

The wise counselor does not harbor a 16-year-old boy or girl in his or her home at 2 a.m. It is definitely not a part of the counselor's job description. Conceivably, a counselor in this situation could be charged with contributing to the delinquency of a minor, a criminal offense. Of course, the ethical counselor does not slam the door in the youth's face either, which might cause considerable emotional trauma. The counselor could encourage the youth to choose between seeking solace in a runaway shelter, calling a help hot line, notifying local law enforcement, or returning home to deal with the problem more directly.

It may seem obvious to state that the counselor must avoid becoming romantically involved with a minor client, but what if a former client is now a legal adult? In a case involving a secondary school counselor who had a sexual encounter with a former client who had recently graduated from high school, a New York appellate court ruled against the counselor and stated that "A professional teacher (counselor) entrusted with forming the moral and social values of our young people must accept the reality that he is held to a high or strict standard of conduct. . ." (*Goldin v. Board of Education*, 1975). The practitioner is warned to avoid any action that could be misinterpreted as a romantic or sexual gesture, including personally flattering compliments, telling dirty jokes, or even questioning a minor's sexual practices. A good rule of thumb to use when considering hugging or touching a client is to allow the client to initiate contact. The counselor should also monitor his or her personal comfort level. The *Ethical Standards* (AACD, 1988) specifically state that "In the counseling relationship, the counselor is aware of the intimacy of the relationship and maintains respect for the client and avoids engaging in activities that seek to meet the counselor's personal needs at the expense of that client."

What if the single parent of a minor client approaches the youth's counselor for a date? If the counselor accepts the proposal, he or she has created a potentially conflicting situation. The child may see this action as a violation of his or her trust—or may welcome the counselor's presence into the family situation. In any case, a counselor's romantic involvement with a minor client's single parent alters the relationship with the child, and so should be avoided. The scenario becomes less clear once the professional relationship with the child has been terminated. Carefully weighing the pros and cons of the situation may give the counselor insight. Consultation with another professional is always a positive practice in uncertain situations.

Occasionally there are conflicts between a parent's values and a child's developing values. If a dual relationship developed in which a counselor became a type of surrogate parent to a minor, in direct opposition to the parent's values and influences, the counselor's actions or inactions could be interpreted by the parent as being obtrusive and a lawsuit could be brought against the counselor for unduly influencing a minor. Mental health professionals have been sued by parents for the interference of a third party in the parent-child relationship, although judgments against counselors are quite rare due to the difficulty of proving damages and causality (Besharov, 1985).

Another possible area of conflict involves receiving gifts from clients. In the school setting, it is not uncommon for counselors to be presented with a small gift at Christmas or on Valentine's Day. Herlihy and Corey (1992) mentioned several factors to consider carefully before accepting a gift: the worth of the item, the client's motivation for giving the gift, the stage of the relationship that has developed, and the motivations of the counselor in accepting or rejecting it. Refusing a child's hand-drawn artwork may conceivably cause more damage to his or her emotional state than accepting it.

By the very age difference of the parties involved, the practice of counseling minor clients lends itself to the possibility of dual relationships being established. The ethical counselor needs to be ever vigilant to the realities of these relationships and to practice in a manner in which minor clients are not harmed.

Records

In 1974, a late amendment to a huge omnibus education funding and busing bill created record confidentiality standards for public school students and their parents. This legislation resulted from a groundswell of organized parent advocacy concerned about invasion of family privacy by school personnel, the unauthorized release of student records to third parties, and access to student records by parents. The Family Educational Rights and Privacy Act of 1974 (also known as FERPA or the Buckley Amendment), 20 U.S.C. 1232 (g) and (h) and related regulations 34 C.F.R. 99.5, were enacted to assure parental access to their children's school records and educational materials. In addition, this Act prohibits release of a student's school records to third parties without parental consent or the student's consent if he or she is 18 years old or attending a postsecondary institution. School records in this context include notes made from interviews conducted by school counselors that are included in a cumulative file accessible to other school personnel. The Act applies to all schools receiving federal education funds, either directly or indirectly.

Some of the most important provisions of 20 U.S.C. 1232 (g) and (h) for counselors who provide services for minors are as follows:

1. Parents have access to educational records of their children. Records must be available within 45 days after request.
2. There must be a procedure in place whereby parents can challenge the content of these records.
3. For the purposes of this Act, education records include files maintained by the institution directly related to a student. Private counseling notes kept in the sole possession of the counselor are not considered educational records.
4. Student records, other than directory information, may not be released without parental consent except to:

   - other school officials with a legitimate educational interest
   - transfer school systems (parent notification required)
   - authorized governmental agencies that audit and monitor compliance with federal funding requirements
   - legitimate research organizations in which the student or parents are not personally identified
   - people involved in health or safety emergency situations
   - parents of a dependent student
   - an officer of the court pursuant to a subpoena (parent and student notification required).

5. Educational institutions must keep a record of every party that has requested or obtained access to a student's records.

The agency regulations in 34 C.F.R. 99.5 that are related to FERPA–20 U.S.C. §1232 (g) and (h)—and important for counselors include the following:

1. Parents or students must be informed annually of their rights regarding school records.
2. Parents and eligible students may inspect and review their records. Proper procedures allowing access, challenging content, and redress of grievances must be formulated and published.
3. A record of those accessing the student's records must be maintained.

It is important to note that biological parents generally have the right to request parent available records, even if the parents were never married, but stepparents do not (Remley, 1990). In addition, noncustodial parents have the right to review their son's or daughter's school records, unless there is a court order directly barring them from doing so. Because school counselors may find themselves in the unwelcome role of policing such parental requests, they should be clear on these regulations.

While administrators and other school personnel originally regarded 20 U.S.C. 1232 (g) and (h) as an unnecessary administrative burden, the passage of time has proven the worth of this legislation. The law has provided both parents and students with legitimate access to student records. The quality and accuracy of student records have improved (Fischer et al., 1987). Perhaps most important, students and their families enjoy improved protection from unwarranted intrusion of their privacy.

Another important area of confidentiality regarding minors' counseling records concerns alcohol and drug abuse patient records. Federal law governs this area of confidentiality. The federal statutes 42 U.S.C. 290 ee–3 and 4582 and subsequent regulations 42 C.F.R. Part 2 govern the treatment of counseling records in a federally funded alcohol or drug abuse treatment setting. In addition to formal treatment programs, these regulations are generally thought to apply to all "federally assisted programs," including state pass-through funds and prevention/early intervention programs in school systems (Western Center, 1989). Although school programs rarely diagnose or treat alcohol or drug abuse dependency, many school counseling programs provide initial assessment services, make referrals, and assist with aftercare plans—all of which fall under the purview of this legislation. The regulations defer to state law when consent to treatment is at issue. If according to state law a minor can independently seek out and consent to substance abuse treatment, then all federal regulations governing treatment records and confidentiality apply just as they do with adults. However, if state law requires consent from both the minor and parent, that law governs all federal provisions for records and releases of information as well.

Under 42 U.S.C. 290 ee–3 and 4582, each service provider must formulate written procedures governing access to records, and all records must be kept in a secure environment. All clients, including minors, must be informed of the substance of this statute and its related regulations, and given a summary in writing. Clients may have access to their records and may obtain copies of them. Records are not released without the proper written consent except:

- to medical personnel for purposes of treating the client in a medical emergency
- in response to a court order issued for good cause
- for licensing or funding source audits, or for qualified personnel conducting scientific research in which individual clients are not personally identified.

Confidentiality and consent are closely related issues when determining the content of records and deciding who may have access to them. Counselors should keep abreast of both federal and state law in these areas and seek competent legal advice when unclear situations arise. Although these laws remain relatively stable and consistent over time, significant changes occur every few years as legislators and courts attempt to respond to new and ever changing conditions.

Frequently Asked Questions

Q. What are the differences between professional records and school records under FERPA?

A. Professional records include, for example, dates of contacts, content of the sessions, general impressions, and reminders for future sessions. As long as these "personal memory" notes are not shown to others (except a paid adult secretary), they are not considered part of school records. They are, however, still subject to the long arm of the law and could be subpoenaed. These counseling notes should never be kept in a student's cumulative education file.

School records (for example, cumulative files and special education records) fall under the Buckley Amendment (FERPA), and there are distinct guidelines for handling these files. The procedures are primarily designed to insure a parent's rights to participate in his or her child's education through knowledge about the information contained in the child's educational record and to assure that personal privacy is maintained.

Q. Under FERPA, do parents have the right to see a counselor's personal notes concerning their son or daughter?

A. No. The FERPA does not give parents the right to review the personal notes of educators covered by the Act (which includes counselors) if these records are in the sole possession of the counselor. However, if these notes have been shared with other school staff members, this protection does not apply.

Q. Can a court require school personnel to disclose a student's counseling records protected under FERPA without parental consent?

A. Probably. In a New York judicial decision, the court held that the FERPA does not prohibit a school from disclosing personally identifiable information concerning a student if it does so pursuant to a court order. In order for parties to obtain such a court order, they must "demonstrate a genuine need for the information that outweighs the privacy interest of the student" (*Rios v. Read*, 1977).

Q. Can parents of a minor client demand access to the professional notes I keep concerning their son or daughter—even if I feel it would be harmful to do so?

A. Parents *probably* have the right to view files kept by a counselor concerning their son or daughter's therapy. A counselor could explain to the parent why he or she prefers not to disclose the notes, object to disclosing the information, or demand to have them subpoenaed, but technically, the notes belong to the client, or in the case of a minor, his or her parents. To avoid legal liability for making libelous statements, it is always wise to label notes of a subjective or speculative nature as such.

Q. If a noncustodial parent shows up at my school office demanding to see school educational records concerning his or her child, can I refuse to disclose them?

A. Probably not. Unless there is a court order barring the noncustodial parent from access to his or her child's records, he or she has the same rights of access to these records as does the custodial parent. A counselor can, however, take a reasonable amount of time to compile and copy the records before disclosing them. Many states allow the school to charge a reasonable fee for the expense involved in providing copies.

Q. Do I need a signed consent to exchange information with another therapist who is working with a minor? Who needs to sign a such a release—the child or the parent?

A. In many states, an exchange of relevant case information among health care providers working actively with the same client does not require a signed consent or release of information. These are states that have adopted the Health Care Information Act, model legislation drafted to achieve uniformity among states concerning health care record-keeping procedures. Check your state statutes. We recommend that a counselor attempt to obtain consent for disclosure from the client and parents regardless of the law. A minor's signature on a release of information form is a positive way of showing you respect his or her privacy. Clients dislike having their counseling record disseminated without their knowledge and consent.

Q. What should I know or do if a custody dispute comes up and I am asked to get involved?

A. Refuse to appear voluntarily. Advocacy for a parent is not a counselor's job. Document all contacts with the client and parents to assure adequate case notes. Obtain signed permission to testify from the minor and parents if possible. A counselor may decide to consult with his or her agency or personal attorney if it is felt that he or she is being placed in a difficult situation. When testifying, speak only to information you know as fact and can support. If asked to give speculative opinions, decline to answer. You might ask the presiding judge if the question is appropriate to respond to. Hope that it all settles out of court.

Q. How do I know if my client is old enough to make an independent decision under the mature minor rule?

A. You will probably need legal advice. If the minor is 14 years or older, has made other important decisions independently, and displays the capacity to make a reasoned decision, a court may grant the minor power to consent, or enforce consent already given by the minor. A legal review of the mature minor statute and cases in the counselor's state will reveal whether or not seeking judicial bypass of parental involvement laws has a reasonable chance for success.

Q. What if I am working with an adult client who tells me he or she was abused as a child (physically or sexually) and it wasn't reported?

A. State child abuse reporting statutes vary greatly. In some states, counselors specifically are required to report past abuse. In other states, the statute does not address past abuse issues. Generally, there is no statute of limitations on abuse, and reports should be made to child protective services or legal authorities, even if your client is now an adult. Rarely is child molestation a one-time incident, and offenders may be abusing other children at the present time.

Guidelines for Practice

When parents disagree about counseling for their child . . .

1. Attempt to schedule a session with one or both parents to discuss and resolve the matter.
2. If the parents are divorced, determine which parent has custody.
3. Determine the motivations of the child. If the child desires counseling despite parental resistance, evaluate using the following questions:
   - How old is the client? The younger the child, the more legal deference is given to the parent's wishes.
   - What is the nature of the presenting problem? Some issues allow the child increased decision-making autonomy (chemical dependency, abortion, certain medical attention).
   - What are the statutes of your state regarding mature minor rules, parental consent, or notification? Seek legal advice if you're unsure about their application.
   - Does parental refusal constitute parental neglect that warrants reporting to local child protective authorities? Will continuing to counsel the child create more problems than it solves?
4. If counseling continues and payment is expected, make sure a fee payment agreement has been signed, preferably by the

consenting parent. Contracts made by minors generally are unenforceable.

5. If you are employed in a school or agency, get support from your supervisor if you decide to counsel the child over one parent's objections.

When you think a minor's consent for treatment or counseling might be necessary or legally permissible . . .

1. Obtain copies of and carefully read all of your state's specific statues concerning the consent of minors for treatment and counseling. Make sure your know the answers to the following questions:

   - Does your state allow minors to consent to therapy in medical and emotional situations?
   - At what age can a minor give consent?
   - Under what circumstances can consent be given?
   - Is abortion referred to in the statute?

2. Consult with an attorney if you are unsure of your legal obligations.

If you are considering an involuntary commitment . . .

1. Obtain copies of and carefully read all of your state's specific statues concerning involuntary commitment. Make sure you know the answers to the following questions:

   - Under what circumstances can a client be committed to a treatment facility or hospital?
   - What steps must be taken to commit a client?
   - Who can determine if a client is in need of involuntary intervention?
   - Must parents give consent?

2. Consult with an attorney if you are unsure of your legal obligations.

When you are pressed by adults to divulge confidential information . . .

1. Ascertain if the child and at least one of the parents wishes the information to be divulged. Remember counseling records are officially the property of the client or, in the case of a minor, the client's parent(s).
2. If the adult is a parent, and you feel that divulging information will be harmful to the child:
   - Explain this to the parent.
   - Schedule a joint session with the child and the parent, hoping that the information will be revealed by the child, or that a compromise can be reached.
   - If the child prefers you not to divulge information, you may decide to refuse to divulge the information, but be prepared to defend your decision in court. Be sure your supervisor supports your decision if you are employed in a school or agency. Does your state have a privileged communication statute? How old is your client?

When you have concerns about privileged communications . . .

1. Find out if your state has a privileged communication statute. If it does, obtain a copy and read it carefully. Make sure you know the answers to the following questions:

   - Are specific professionals named?
   - Is the privilege all encompassing or are there exceptions specifically listed, for example, in instances of child abuse or if the courts order the privilege waived?

2. Consult with an attorney if you are unsure of your legal obligations.

When you suspect child abuse or neglect . . .

1. Obtain copies of and carefully read all of your state's statues in this area. Because state child abuse statutes vary considerably, it is important for you to consider the exact language. Make sure you know the answers to the following questions:

   - Who is required to report?
   - What types of abuse are specifically defined?

- To whom does a counselor report suspected abuse?
- Is a written report necessary or will a phone call suffice?

2. Consult with an attorney if you are uncertain about your legal obligations.
3. Consider as criteria for reporting child abuse or neglect:

- a child's report of being abused or neglected
- direct observation of a parent's abusive or neglectful behavior
- a parent's description or admission of abusive or neglectful behavior
- a child's injuries that suggest direct physical abuse or that result from the child's exposure to unwarranted dangerous situations
- evidence of parental impairment that renders child abuse or neglect likely
- parental neglect of a child's physical injuries
- collateral reports of abuse or neglect (from other family members, neighbors, the child's friends) that appear to have substantial basis in fact
- evidence that the parent has abandoned care of the child.

If a minor girl seeks pregnancy or abortion counseling . . .

1. Suggest that the child obtain valid pregnancy and HIV tests.
2. Determine how much parental involvement the child has sought or wishes to include. Your main function may be to facilitate notification of parents.
3. Know your state abortion and adoption statutes, particularly their application to minors. Assist your client in seeking legal advice if necessary.
4. Create a referral list of relevant resources, including abortion and adoption providers, teenage pregnancy service providers, legal resources for judicial bypass, and counseling services specific to abortion and adoption.
5. Do not advocate for either abortion or adoption! This is not your decision to make. If your values interfere with providing objective assistance, make a referral.

If you are considering exercising the duty to warn . . .

1. Obtain copies of and carefully read all of your state's specific statues relating to the duty to warn. Make sure you know the answers to the following questions:
   - Does the statute define the steps that must be taken to fulfill a professional's duty to warn?
   - Is it clear who should be contacted?
   - How specific must the threat be before a counselor should act to protect individuals or society?
2. Consult with an attorney if you are uncertain about your legal obligations.
3. Consider as criteria for exercising the duty to warn:
   - a specific threat toward an identified or reasonably identified person
   - a threat that includes a description of the means of intended harm
   - a present ability to carry out the intended harm
   - a general pattern of violent or abusive behavior, especially when under the influence of alcohol or other drugs
   - a history of physical abuse between the client and intended victim.

If you find yourself in a situation in which a dual relationship might occur . . .

1. Avoid the dual relationship if at all possible. For example, refer minor clients to other professionals or remove yourself from the conflicting role.
2. If a dual relationship is not avoidable, weigh the potential benefits against the possible harm to both the client and yourself. Will your role of counselor be compromised?
3. Inform your minor clients of the inherent limits to confidentiality and the helping relationship at the outset of counseling. Address dual relationship concerns immediately and directly as they develop.
4. Educate your coworkers and supervisors as to your job description and responsibilities. Object to being placed in roles that negatively impact your helping role.
5. Maintain a professional distance with your clients and their families. Avoid becoming overly involved in their private lives or fostering a dependency on you as a helper.

6. Consult with other professionals to assist your ability to maintain objectivity.

Summary

Counselors must recognize that there are few black and white answers to the complex legal and ethical situations that arise when counseling child and adolescent clients. The legal rights of minors, parents, professionals, agencies, and society all compete when vying for the child's best interest, and much gray area exists.

In general, minors' rights are vested in their parents. The courts follow the precept that parents have the major responsibility of knowing what is best for their child. This is especially true for younger children. Around the age of 14, juveniles begin to exert more personal influence in legal matters. For example, teenagers are routinely asked their opinion in custody cases. In certain circumstances (abortion, chemical dependency, sexually transmitted diseases) minors enjoy greater autonomy in their decision making. Specific federal statutes and state laws provide exceptions to the usual necessary parental involvement. A counselor is urged to consult his or her state's statutes in these areas.

Know and follow the ethical guidelines applicable to your profession. These guidelines provide the professional standards of practice by which you are judged in a court of law. Consulting with other professionals is a best practice that helps to insure that you are acting as others in your field would. Consulting with an attorney familiar with mental health issues and juvenile law is a necessity when faced with the realities of legal proceedings, either as a witness or defendant.

Because of the evolving complexity of our world, minors today face an ever increasing array of difficult issues and are in need of counseling services more than ever. Despite potential legal liabilities and gray areas, counseling minor clients continues to be one of the most rewarding endeavors for human services professionals.

Discussion Questions

1. What are the legal differences between adults and minors? At what age or stage of development do minors begin to assume adult rights and responsibilities? What are the relevant statutes in your state of residence? Do variations exist for specific situations such as pregnancy and abortion counseling or chemical dependency treatment?

2. A parent has become increasingly concerned about the effects of your counseling sessions on her 13-year-old child. Finally, she decides that the child is better off without your services. If the child comes to you wishing to continue counseling, what will you do?

3. The divorced mother and father of an 11-year-old girl disagree regarding their daughter's need for counseling. Both parents share custody, the mother and child want the counseling, and you agree that counseling is needed. Unfortunately, the court decree stipulates that the father will pay all medical expenses, including any counseling fees. Will you accept this client for counseling? If so, how will you assure that you are paid for your services?

4. Suppose you have been seeing a minor for divorce adjustment counseling at the request of the child's mother, whom you have seen in sessions with the child. The father, who has joint

custody rights, now schedules an appointment with you. In the session, the father presses you for information about the relationship between the mother and child. He states adamantly that he has the right to review your counseling notes concerning his child. How do you respond?

5. How does a counselor's job setting affect the way he or she approaches a request to counsel a minor client? What attitudes or perceptions toward children and adolescent clients does a counselor develop in the work setting? How might these perceptions bias a mental health professional who changes work settings?

6. How might a school counselor prioritize his or her duties and responsibilities to students, parents, administrators, the school or district, and society when there are conflicting needs or desires? In what situations could a school counselor find himself or herself being pulled in two opposite directions concerning a minor client? How should one go about resolving opposing demands, or avoiding them in the first place?

7. In a group counseling setting developed to explore positive lifestyles, one of the members (a minor) states that he or she "gets high" with his or her mother. Upon further exploration, the minor reveals that his or her mother provides the marijuana. Should the counselor report this to the local child protective services or legal authorities? Does the age of the minor make a difference? Suppose the drug was heroin, or crack cocaine.

8. As a high school counselor, you have designed a voluntary contemporary affairs group to be held at school after normal school hours. Under FERPA, do you need to obtain consent forms signed by a parent?

9. During one group session a group member discloses that his father, now divorced from the child's mother and a noncustodial parent, is gay. One week later, the father storms into your office demanding to see your group notes because stories about his sexual preference have been circulating among his business associates. Under FERPA must you disclose your group notes?

10. A 16-year-old girl comes into your office and discloses that she is pregnant. She wishes to get an abortion and is horrified by the prospect of notifying her parents. She has heard that other girls have gone to court to obtain permission to get an abortion without parental involvement, and she wants to do that. As her counselor, how will you proceed?

11. Is it possible for a counselor to work with a minor client and not develop a dual relationship based on the natural adult-child dichotomy? What precautions does a counselor need to take to avoid being looked up to or emulated by a child or young adult? How does one maintain a professional distance in close relationships with minors?

Suggested Readings

Besharov, D.J. (1985). *The vulnerable social worker: Liability for serving children and families*. Silver Spring, MD: National Association of Social Workers. Contains informative sections on reporting suspected child abuse and neglect, and reducing legal vulnerability.

Herlihy, B., & Corey, G. (1992). *Dual relationships in counseling*. Alexandria, VA: American Association for Counseling and Development. Explores the ethical and legal complexities of dual relationships in a variety of settings.

Hopkins, B.R., & Anderson, B.S. (1990). *The counselor and the law* (3rd ed.). Alexandria, VA: American Association for Counseling and Development. Covers several general topics. Contains sections on civil and criminal liability of counselors plus business practice issues.

Huey, W.C., & Remley T.P. Jr., Eds. (1989). *Ethical and legal issues in school counseling*. Alexandria, VA: American Association for Counseling and Development. Provides a clear distinction between ethical and legal duties in the school setting. Excellent sections on court testimony, educational testing, and confidentiality.

Hummel, D.L., Talbutt, L.C., & Alexander, M.D. (1985). *Law and ethics in counseling*. New York: Van Nostrand Reinhold. A thorough examination of the legal system as it relates to the counseling field with many citations of relevant court cases.

References

Alabama Code Ann. 22-8-4 through 6 (1984).
American Association for Counseling and Development. (1988). *Ethical standards*. Alexandria, VA: Author.
American Bar Association, Institute of Judicial Administration. (1980). *Rights of minors*. Cambridge, MA: Ballenger.
Belotti v. Baird, 433 U.S. 622 (1979).
Besharov, D.J. (1985). *The vulnerable social worker: Liability for serving children and families*. Silver Spring, MD: National Association of Social Workers.
Besharov, D.J. (1988). Child abuse and neglect reporting and investigation: Policy guidelines for decision making. *Family Law Quarterly, 22*(1), 1–15.
Bullis, R.K. (1992). "*Law and management of a counseling agency or private practice.*" ACA Legal Series, Vol. 3. Alexandria, VA: American Association for Counseling and Development.
Cambin, L.D., & Prout, H.T. (1983). School counselors and the reporting of child abuse: A survey of state laws and practices. *School Counselor 30*, 358–367.
Carey v. Population Servs. Int'l., 431 U.S. 678 (1977).
Croxton, T.A., Churchill, S.R., & Fellin, P. (1988). Counseling minors without parental consent. *Child Welfare, 67*(1), 3–14.
DeBruyn, R.L. (1991). Crossing the line from teacher to buddy. *The Master Teacher, 23*(4).
Family Educational Rights and Priving Act of 1974, 20 U.S.C. §1232 (g) & (h) (1974). 34 C.F.R. 99.5.

Federal Drug and Alcohol Confidentiality Act of 1987, 42 U.S.C. 290 ee-3 and 4582 (1987). 42 C.F.R. Part 2.

Fischer, L., Schimmel, D., & Kelly, C. (1987). *Teachers and the law*. New York: Longman.

Goldin v. Board of Education, 357 N.Y.S. 2d 867 (1975).

Groff v. State of Florida, 390 S.2d 368 (2nd D.C. Fla. 1980).

Herlihy, B., & Corey, G. (1992). *Dual relationships in counseling*. Alexandria, VA: American Association for Counseling and Development.

H.L. v. Matheson, 450 U.S. 398,101 S.Ct. 1164, 67 L.Ed.2d 388 (1981).

Horowitz, R., & Davidson, H. (1984). *Legal rights of children*. New York: McGraw Hill.

Hopkins, B.R., & Anderson, B.S. (1990). *The counselor and the law* (3rd ed.). Alexandria, VA: American Association for Counseling and Development.

Hummel, D.L., Talbutt, L.C., & Alexander, M.D. (1985). *Law and ethics in counseling*. New York: Van Nostrand Reinhold.

In re E.G., 549 N.E.2d. 322 (1989).

Landeros v. Flood, 551 P.2d 368, (S.C. Calif. 1976).

McIntosh v. Milano, 403 A2d. 500 (1979).

Meyer, R.G., Landis, E.R., & Hays, J.R. (1988). *Law for the psychotherapist*. New York: W.W. Norton.

Montana Code Annotated, 41-3-201 (1991).

National Abortion Federation. (1991). *Parental involvement laws; a guide for abortion providers*. Washington, DC: Author.

Newburgh v. Arrigo, 443 A.2d. 1031 (1982).

Niesen v. Niesen, 157 N.W. 2d. 660 (1968).

Peck v. Counseling Services of Addison County, Inc., 499 A2d. 422 (Vt.1985).

Perira v. U.S., 74 S.Ct. 358 (1974).

Planned Parenthood of Southeastern Pennsylvania v. Casey, 60 U.S.L.W. 4795 (June 30, 1992).

Remley, T.P., Jr. (1990). *Safeguarding against ethical and legal danger points*. Ann Arbor, MI: ERIC/CAPS Workshop.

Remley, T.P., Jr. (1991). *"Preparing for court appearances."* ACA Legal Series, Vol. 1. Alexandria, VA: American Counseling Association. (Originally published by American Association for Counseling and Development as the AACD Legal Series.)

Rios v. Read, 73 F.R.D. 589 (E.D.N.Y. 1977).

Roe v. Wade, 410 U.S. 113 (1973).

Roman v. Appleby, 558 F, Supp. 449 (E.D. Pa. 1983).
Salo, M., & Shumate, S. (1991). *Common legal and ethical concerns of school counselors in Montana: An informational brochure*. Bozeman, MT: Montana School Counselor Association.
Schutz, B.M. (1986). *Legal liability in psychotherapy*. San Francisco: Jossey-Bass.
Sheeley, V.L., & Herlihy, B. (1987). Privileged communication in school counseling: Status update. *The School Counselor, 34*, 268–272.
Tarasoff v. Regents of Univ. of Calif., 551 P.2d. 334 (Cal. 1976).
Wadlington, W. (1973). Minors and health care: The age of consent. *Osgood Hall Law Journal, 11*, 115–125.
Webster v. Reproductive Services, 109 S.Ct. 3040 (1989).
Western Center Drug-Free Schools and Communities. (1989). *Confidentiality of student records*. Portland, OR: Author.
Younts v. St. Francis Hospital, 469 P.2d. 330 (1970).

Representative mature minor state statutes that include provisions regarding independent access to medical and mental health services:

Alabama Code Ann. 22-8-4 through 6 (1975).
California Civ. Code 34.5 through 34.6 (1992).
Colorado Rev. Stat. 13-22-102 through 105 (1989).
Virginia Code Ann. 54.1 - 2969 (1991).

NOTES

NOTES

NOTES